HOUGHTON MIFFLIN
Reading

Amazing
Animals

 HOUGHTON MIFFLIN

BOSTON

ISBN 0-618-38722-6

5 6 7 8 9 10-BS-12 11 10 09 08 07 06 05

Design, Art Management, and Page Production: Silver Editions.

Contents

A Park for Parkdale

by Patty Moynahan

illustrated by Bethann Thornburgh

Parkdale is a very nice town. It has houses and farms and stores. It has a market that sells nearly everything. It is a fine town, except for one thing. Parkdale has no park.

At the town meeting, Bart Horn stood up. "I have something important to say this morning," he told the town board. "We feel that a town named Parkdale needs a park."

Doctor Short nodded. So did Miss Martin.

"Pardon me," said Cora Barkway, "but how will we pay for this park? We will need land. We will need someone to tend to this park."

The people began to think. Then Bart had an idea.

"Listen!" said Bart. "We will work together to make this park."

The people liked this smart plan.

"We'll start right now!" said Bart.

"I know a good spot for our park."

Bart led everyone to an old, weedy lot. "Let's make a park!" he shouted.

Doctor Short and others cleaned up trash. Miss Martin planted a garden. More and more people came to help.

On March first, Parkdale Park opened. People ate and played and had fun. The mayor made a speech.

He said, "We are proud. See what can happen when everyone helps out!"

Parkdale is a very nice town. It
has houses and farms and stores
and a market.

And now it has a park!

Arthur's Book

by Patty Moynahan
illustrated by John Manders

Arthur wanted to write his own
book. He had stacks and stacks of nice
white paper. He had three new pens.
He had lots of time for writing. Just
one thing was missing.

Arthur needed an idea. He started
thinking and thinking.

"I'll tell a tale about a frightful sea
creature," he told himself. "It could be
a mixture of fact and fiction."

Arthur looked out the window. He
saw his cat chasing his dog.

"How will this sea creature act?" he
asked. "That's the question."

Arthur kept thinking and thinking.

Outside, his dog jumped up a tree.
Arthur did not see.

"My brain is starting to hurt," said
Arthur. "How hard can it be to get
an idea?"

Then Arthur looked back outside. He saw his cat run up the tree. He saw his dog in the tree. It was very funny.

"Sea creatures do not do funny things like that!" Arthur said. "I need a new idea."

Arthur felt that it might be helpful
to look at books. He picked up a book
from the fiction section of his shelf.
Just then, his dog and cat raced by.
They made him drop his book. That got
his attention.

14

"That's it!" he yelled. He had an idea.

"My story will be about a cat that chases a dog. I know about that!" he said.

Then he went back to his desk and started to write.

Hank's Pandas

by Linda Dunlap
illustrated by Teri Sloat

My big brother is named Hank. He
takes care of pandas at Animal Park.
Hank tells me stories about his work. If
I want, he takes me to see his pandas.

Hank begins his work day by feeding the pandas. Zoo pandas eat foods that wild pandas eat. They chomp on plants.

18

Then Hank might weigh the new
baby. It is so small! Hank can hold it in
his arms.

Between his chores, Hank just
watches the pandas. He likes to think
and learn about pandas. Hank tells me
what he sees.

20

Mom and her baby drink pond water.
Dad sits close by.

Pandas have nice fur. They groom it
every day. Their light parts look as
clean as snow.

Mom cleans baby panda. Dad lends a
hand. Then they go to sleep.

Hank and I go away quietly. We will
be back to see the pandas soon.

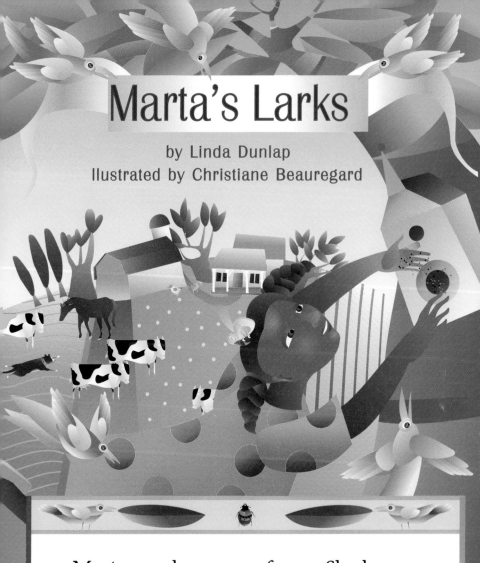

Marta's Larks

by Linda Dunlap
Illustrated by Christiane Beauregard

Marta was born on a farm. She has
chores every day. The chore she likes best is
feeding larks. Larks are birds that sing a lot.
Marta likes to hear them each day.

25

In March, Marta works in her garden.
She sees larks try teamwork to turn a leaf.
"What is under that leaf?" Marta thinks.

Marta picks up the leaf. A fat bug looks back at her! "Wow! Those larks are smart!" exclaims Marta. "I will start watching larks at work."

Marta sees larks working hard finding food. Even little larks eat lots of bugs. Larks swoop and dart in the sky. Hardly any bugs get away!

Marta sees larks working hard making nests. Larks pull bits of bark from large trees. They take blades of grass from the yard. Larks find torn yarn. They carry these things to a safe place. Then larks turn bark, grass, and yarn into nests!

29

Marta likes watching larks at work. And larks feel safe when Marta is close. Marta would never harm her larks!

Marta is a part of her larks' life. Larks
perch on her arms. Others eat seeds from
her hands. Marta is glad to have larks for
friends.

31

Crow's Plan

by Melissa Blackwell Burke
illustrated by Cary Phillips

The animals at Oak Lake had a big problem. They met in the field to speak about it.

"Long ago, Oak Lake flowed clean," said Crow. "Now trash floats in it. We must make this lake flow clean once more."

"How can we help?" Toad croaked.

"We will make war on trash. Follow me!" said Crow.

Half the animals went around one side of Oak Lake. The rest went around the other side. They picked up trash and put it in trash cans.

"This lake looks good and clean," Toad croaked. "Let's keep it this way."

"We can wait in this hollow tree," Crow said. "Then we will show everyone how to take care of the lake. It must be our goal."

Soon a raccoon family came to Oak Lake. The family ate a picnic in their rowboat. When they finished, the little raccoon tossed something. In a flash, Crow dove and got that trash in his beak before it hit Oak Lake.

Crow dropped that trash in a trash
can. He flew back and bellowed at that
family.

"I think I know why Crow is mad," the
dad explained. "We won't throw trash
again, fellow," he yelled up at Crow.

Crow went back to the hollow tree
and spoke with the animals. "This is
how we will show everyone. It must be
our goal."

"Yes," they said. "You have our oath.
If we see someone throw trash, we will
croak or moan or bellow."

So when you hear animals croak or
moan or bellow, think about this tale.
And don't throw trash!

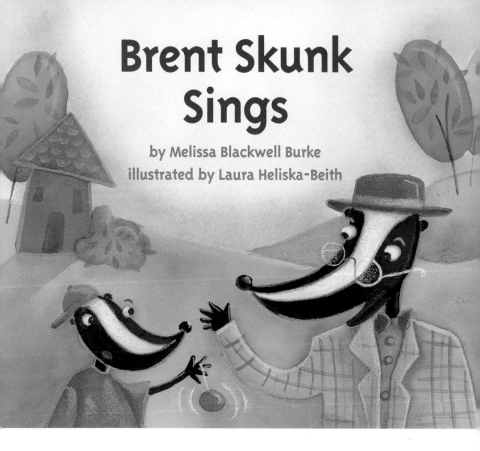

Brent Skunk Sings

by Melissa Blackwell Burke

illustrated by Laura Heliska-Beith

It was time for Brent Skunk to make his first trip to the dentist.

"This bird is the best dentist in this land," Granddad Frank said. "He is quite nice. When we go, he will clean your teeth and check them out. It will not hurt a bit."

Brent Skunk was afraid.

"This dentist visit won't take long," Granddad Frank said. "And you can bring that yo-yo you like so much."

So Brent Skunk and Granddad Frank went down to the dentist.

Brent Skunk and Granddad Frank sat in the waiting room.

When it was time to see the dentist, Granddad Frank found Brent Skunk behind a plant.

Granddad Frank yanked Brent Skunk out.

Granddad Frank set Brent Skunk
down. Brent Skunk slumped.

Just then, the dentist came in.

"Brent Skunk, you'll be fine. We'll
just count and clean and check those
teeth. Let me get my lamp on so we
can see. Open wide, please."

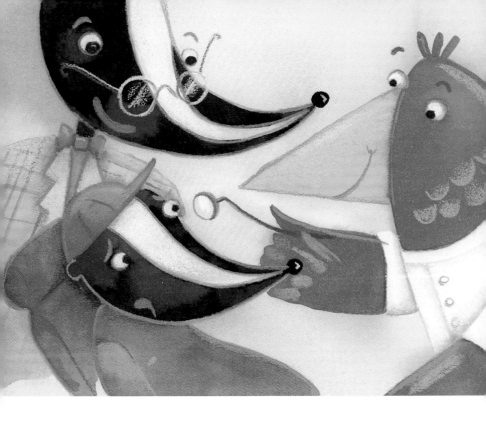

But Brent Skunk kept his mouth closed tight. He just sat there blinking.

"We'll get you a new toy with a string when we are through," the dentist said. "Now please open up."

Brent Skunk still kept his mouth closed tight.

"This skunk has me stumped!" the dentist said. "What do you think we can try, Frank?"

"He opens wide when he laughs. We need to make him laugh. Can you do a stunt with that yo-yo?" Granddad Frank asked.

The dentist did three stunts. And Brent Skunk laughed, but with his hand over his mouth.

46

"I've got it!" Granddad Frank said. "Brent can't pass up a chance to sing. How about it, Brent?"

So Brent Skunk sang, and opened wide.

The dentist counted and cleaned and checked Brent's teeth.

It did not hurt a bit.

Where Do I Start?

by Sarah Amada

illustrated by Christine Beauregard

Something was wrong. I had to write a biography. I couldn't think of anyone to write about. I had no idea what to say.

"I don't know where to start," I said. "I'm stumped!"

"Think of someone brave or with a special talent," said Dad. "Is there someone you know with a neat job?"

I thought and thought. "I could write about your friend Mr. Parks!" I said.

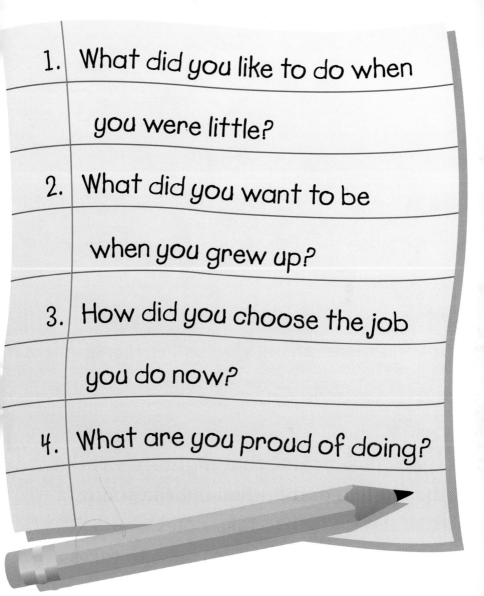

1. What did you like to do when you were little?

2. What did you want to be when you grew up?

3. How did you choose the job you do now?

4. What are you proud of doing?

Dad called Mr. Parks. I wrote down many of my questions.

Mr. Parks came that night. We sat in the kitchen and I asked my questions. I used a notebook to take notes.

I already knew that Mr. Parks takes pictures of sea animals. I found out that he lives on the seacoast and goes to work on a boat.

When he was a boy, Mr. Parks liked to watch ocean animals. Now he takes pictures of creatures like sea horses, whales, and sharks. His pictures can be seen in nature books and magazines.

Mr. Parks told me many stories. Once he saw a large, dark bump on the ocean floor. At first he thought it was a sandbar. Then he thought it could be a monster. As he got closer, he saw that it was a sunken ship!

We talked and talked. Before Mr.
Parks left, I thanked him for his help.

When he was gone, I groaned loudly.
"What's wrong now?" asked my dad.

"I took so many notes," I said. "I'll
need to give my hand a rest before
I start!"

Word List

A Park for Parkdale **(p. 1)** accompanies *Officer Buckle and Gloria.*

DECODABLE WORDS

Target Skills
r-Controlled Vowel *ar*
Barkway, Bart, farms, garden, March, market, Martin, pardon, park, Parkdale, smart, start

r-Controlled Vowels *or, ore*
Cora, Doctor, for, Horn, important, mayor, more, morning, Short, stores

Words Using Previously Taught Skills
an, and, at, ate, but, came, can, cleaned, did, everything, except, feel, fine, first, fun, good, had, happen, has, he, help, helps, houses, how, is, it, know, land, led, let's, liked, lot, made, make, me, meeting, Miss, named, need, needs, nice, no, nodded, now, on, opened, out, pay, plan, planted, played, proud, right, say, see, sells, shouted, so, speech, spot, stood, tend, that, then, thing, think, this, town, trash, up, we, weedy, we'll, when, will

HIGH-FREQUENCY WORDS

New
board, listen, told

Previously Taught
a, are, began, everyone, have, I, idea, nearly, old, one, opened, others, our, people, said, someone, something, the, to, together, very, what, work

Arthur's Book **(p. 9)** accompanies *Officer Buckle and Gloria.*

DECODABLE WORDS

Target Skill (Review)
Common Syllables *–tion, –ture*
attention, fiction, section, creature, creatures, mixture

Words Using Previously Taught Skills
about, act, an, and, Arthur, asked, at, back, be, book, books, brain, by, can, cat, chases, chasing, desk, did, dog, drop, fact, felt, for, frightful, from, funny, get, got, had, hard, he, helpful, him, himself, his, how, hurt, in, is, it, jumped, just, kept, know, look, looked, lots, made, might, missing, my, need, needed, new, out, outside, own, not, pens, picked, question, raced, run, saw, sea, see, shelf, stacks, started, starting, story, tale, tell, that, that's, then, thing, things, thinking, this, three, time, tree, up, went, white, will, write, writing, yelled

HIGH-FREQUENCY WORDS

Previously Taught
a, could, do, I, idea, of, one, paper, said, the, they, to, told, very, wanted, was

Hank's Pandas (p. 17) accompanies *Ant.*

DECODABLE WORDS

Target Skills
Words with *nd, nt, mp, ng, nk*
chomp, drink, hand, Hank, Hank's, kingdom, lends, panda, pandas, plants, pond

Base Words and Endings -*s*, -*es*, -*ies*
chores, foods, parts, sees, stories, takes, tells

Words Using Previously Taught Skills
and, animal, arms, as, at, away, baby, back, be, big, by, can, clean, cleans, close, dad, day, eat, feeding, for, fur, go, groom, he, her, his, if, in, is, it, just, light, likes, look, me, might, mom, my, named, new, nice, on, park, quietly, see, sits, sleep, snow, so, soon, that, then, tree, we, wild, will, with, zoo

HIGH-FREQUENCY WORDS

New
between, care, weigh

Previously Taught
a, about, begins, brother, every, have, hold, I, learn, small, the, their, they, think, to, want, watches, water, what, work

Marta's Larks (p. 25) accompanies *Ant.*

DECODABLE WORDS

Target Skill (Review)
r-Controlled Vowels *-ar, -or, -ore*

arms, bark, born, chore, chores, dart, farm, garden, hard, hardly, harm, large, larks, larks', March, Marta, Marta's, part, smart, start, torn, yard, yarn

Words Using Previously Taught Skills

and, at, ate, back, best, big, birds, bits, blades, bug, bugs, by, close, day, each, eat, every, exclaims, fat, feeding, feel, felt, find, finding, food, for, from, get, glad, grass, hands, her, in, is, leaf, likes, looks, lot, lots, making, nests, on, perch, picks, place, safe, seeds, sees, she, sky, swoop, take, that, them, then, these, things, thinks, those, trees, try, turn, up, when, will, wow

HIGH-FREQUENCY WORDS

Previously Taught

a, any, are, away, even, friends, has, have, hear, I, into, little, never, of, others, pull, the, they, to, under, was, watching, what, work, works, working, would

Crow's Plan (p. 33) accompanies *The Great Ball Game.*

Target Skill
Vowel Pairs *oa, ow*
bellow, bellowed, croak, croaked, Crow, fellow, floats, flow, flowed, follow, goal, hollow, know, moan, Oak, oath, rowboat, show, slow, throw, Toad

Words Using Previously Taught Skills
about, and, animals, around, at, ate, be, before, big, back, beak, came, can, cans, care, carry, clean, dad, don't, dove, dropped, everyone, family, finished, flash, flew, for, good, got, had, he, help, his, hit, how, if, in, is, it, keep, lake, let's, little, looks, mad, make, me, met, more, must, my, now, on, other, picked, picnic, problem, put, raccoon, rest, saw, see, side, so, soon, speak, spoke, take, tale, that, this, then, think, tossed, trash, tree, up, wait, way, we, went, when, why, will, with, won't, yelled, yes, you

New
ago, field, half, war

Previously Taught
a, about, again, have, hear, I, long, of, once, one, or, our, said, the, their, they, to

Brent Skunk Sings (p. 41) accompanies *The Great Ball Game.*

Target Skill (Review)
Words with *nd, nt, mp, ng, nk*
and, behind, blinking, Brent, Brent's, bring, count, counted, dentist, found, Frank, Granddad, hand, lamp, land, plant, sang, sing, Skunk, slumped, string, stumped, stunt, stunts, think, went, yanked

Words Using Previously Taught Skills
about, asked, be, best, bird, bit, but, came, can, can't, chance, check, checked, clean, cleaned, closed, did, down, fine, for, get, go, got, had, has, he, him, his, how, hurt, is, it, I've, just, kept, let, like, listen, make, me, mouth, much, my, need, new, nice, not, on, opened, opens, out, over, pass, please, quite, room, sat, set, so, see, still, take, teeth, that, them, then, this, those, three, tight, time, toy, trip, try, up, visit, waiting, we, we'll, when, wide, with, will, won't, you, you'll, yo-yo

HIGH-FREQUENCY WORDS

Previously Taught
a, afraid, are, behind, do, first, in, laugh, laughed, laughs, long, open, said, the, there, through, to, was, what, your

DECODABLE WORDS

Target Skills (Review)

r-Controlled Vowels *ar, or, ore*

before, born, dark, horses, large, Mr. Parks, sandbar, sharks, start

Final Syllables and Endings *-ed, -er, -est, -ing, -ly, -tion, -ture*

asked, called, closer, creatures, doing, groaned, liked, loudly, nature, pictures, questions, stumped, talked, thanked, used

Words Using Previously Taught Skills

animals, anyone, as, at, be, boat, books, boy, brave, bump, came, can, choose, clipboard, couldn't, dad, did, didn't, don't, got, grew, had, has, help, him, his, how, I'll, I'm, job, knew, left, lives, magazines, meet, monster, need, neat, night, no, notes, pick, proud, rest, sat, say, sea, seacoast, seen, ship, someone, sunken, take, talent, that, them, think, thought, tired, watch, whales, what's, when, with, wrong, wrote

HIGH-FREQUENCY WORDS

Previously Taught

a, about, all, already, and, are, before, could, do, down, have, I, in, is, it, first, floor, for, found, friend, give, goes, gone, hand, he, idea, kitchen, know, like, little, live, many, me, my, ocean, of, on, once, or, out, now, said, saw, so, something, special, stories, the, there, to, told, too, up, want, was, we, were, what, where, who, work, would, write, you

GENRE VOCABULARY WORDS

biography

62

HIGH-FREQUENCY WORDS TAUGHT TO DATE:

Grade 1	car	found	like	piece	though	Grade 2	reason
a	carry	four	little	play	thoughts	across	roll
able	caught	friend	live	present	three	ago	soldier
about	children	full	long	pretty	through	beautiful	special
above	climb	funny	look	pull	tiny	behind	stand
afraid	cold	garden	love	put	to	believe	story
after	color	girl	many	read	today	between	straight
again	come	give	me	ready	together	board	surprise
against	could	go	minute	right	too	bought	told
all	cow	goes	more	room	try	brother	touch
already	dance	gone	morning	said	turn	brought	until
also	divide	good	most	saw	two	busy	war
always	do	green	mother	school	under	care	weigh
and	does	grow	my	second	upon	clothes	whole
animal	done	happy	near	see	very	different	winter
any	door	hard	never	seven	walk	during	word
are	down	have	not	shall	wall	even	year
arms	draw	he	now	sharp	want	field	young
around	eat	head	ocean	she	warm	floor	
away	edge	hear	of	shoe(s)	was	front	
baby	eight	her	off	shout	wash	great	
bear	else	here	old	show	watched	guess	
because	enough	hold	on	sing	water	half	
been	evening	horse	once	small	we	heard	
before	ever	house	one	so	wear	important	
began	every	how	only	some	were	kitchen	
begin	fall	hungry	open	soon	what	lady	
bird	family	hurt	or	start	where	later	
blue	far	I	other	sure	who	letter	
body	father	idea	our	table	why	lion	
both	find	in	out	talk	work	listen	
break	first	is	over	tall	world	move	
brown	five	jump	own	teacher	would	order	
build	flower	kind	paper	the	write	poor	
butter	fly	know	part	their	you	quiet	
buy	follow	laugh	people	there	your		
by	for	learn	person	these			
call	forest	light	picture	they			

Decoding Skills Taught to Date: Short Vowels *a, i;* Base Words and Endings *-s, -ed, -ing;* Short Vowels *o, u, e;* VCCV Pattern; Long Vowels *a, i* (CVC*e*); Long Vowels *o, u, e* (CVC*e*); Two Sounds for *g;* Consonant Clusters *r, l, s;* Two Sounds for *c;* Double Consonants; VCV Pattern; Final *k* and *ck;* Consonant Digraphs *th, wh, sh, ch, (tch);* Base Words and Endings *-er, -est;* Vowel Pairs *ai, ay;* Compound Words; Vowel Pairs *ow, ou;* Suffixes *-ly, -ful;* Vowel Pairs *ee, ea;* Common Syllables *-tion, -ture;* r-Controlled Vowels *ar, or, ore;* Words with *nd, nt, mp, ng, nk;* Base Words and Endings *-s, -es, -ies;* Vowel Pairs *oa, ow;* Final Syllables and Endings; r- Controlled Vowels